5 THINGS ANYONE CAN DO TO

INTRODUCE OTHERS TO JESUS

D1564862

5 THINGS ANYONE CAN DO TO

INTRODUCE OTHERS TO JESUS

CHRIS CONRAD

wesleyan
publishing
house

Indianapolis, Indiana

CONTENTS

INTRODUCTION

Imagine with me that your favorite group is performing a concert in your town, or perhaps your favorite play or musical is coming. To attend at all would increase your heart rate with great anticipation. But you're not just attending, you're sitting in the front row! You will have the very best seats in the house. It will be a night you'll talk about for weeks, even months, afterwards. Who knows, it might even create a lifelong memory. Nothing would be able to dampen your excitement on that day.

There are moments in life and then there are defining moments—times when life takes on a whole new dimension and we feel fully alive. What if I told you God wants to give you a front row seat to the most dynamic and exciting event that occurs in the universe? Would you believe me? It's true. The Holy Spirit wants to usher you into the seats God has specifically planned for you to witness in the greatest adventure being played out in history.

Unfortunately, a vast majority of Christians choose to turn down the Holy Spirit's invitation. Sounds crazy, doesn't it? Unless someone died or landed in the hospital, we would do everything possible to attend a concert we had front row seats to, yet when God invites us to be His special guest, we come up with a litany of excuses.

Let me be clear. On a regular basis the Holy Spirit invites us to join Him in the grand adventure of introducing people to a Heavenly Father who stands ready to fully forgive everything they've ever done wrong and usher them into an eternity of doing life with the One who created them.

If you've ever joined the Holy Spirit in His ongoing work, then you know firsthand the absolute joy of sensing that you are being used by the Savior to bring someone to Him. When we get to heaven, the days we will remember the most here on earth are not anniversaries, birthdays, graduations, or even the births of our children. We will remember the day we ourselves came into a relationship with Christ and any day we joined the Holy Spirit in bringing others to Him. Those days will be the highlights of our time on earth.

"But Chris, I'm *not* an evangelist." I have heard this excuse countless times. I can relate to it; neither am I! For two years while I interned in my home-church, I worked for someone who had the spiritual gift of evangelism. Not only did he enjoy sharing his faith on a regular basis, but he was also great at it. He was continually striking up spiritual conversations with total strangers and sharing the gospel with them, often resulting in the person coming to Christ. Although I spent many hours with this individual and went on many "soul winning" appointments in those two years, my overall discomfort with "cold turkey" evangelism didn't change much. In fact, if you know you have the spiritual gift of evangelism, don't waste your time reading this book, just get out there and do what you are naturally gifted to do. This book is for those who are convinced that evangelism is *not* their gift.

Many Christians live within this terrible dichotomy. On one hand we know we need to be obedient to the Great Commission given in Matthew 28:19–20: "Therefore, go

9

and make disciples of all the nations, baptizing them in the name of the Father and the Son and the Holy Spirit. Teach these new disciples to obey all the commands I have given you. And be sure of this: I am with you always, even to the end of the age," but we feel utterly inadequate for the task. I'm convinced the reason why such a high percentage of people do not share their faith is because we approach evangelism from the wrong direction. Instead of seeing evangelism as something the Holy Spirit does naturally through us, we feel like it's something we do on our own. We somehow think it's all up to us—and that's just not the case.

Jesus would never have asked us to do something we were incapable of doing. Introducing others to a transformed life was never meant to be reserved for the "spiritual elite." *All* of us who call ourselves Christians have been commissioned and empowered to join Him in bringing others to eternal life. *You can do this!* Regardless of personality! Regardless of how outgoing or shy you are! You can experience God using you in ways that will leave you speechless with amazement. This is a crucial aspect of the abundant life Jesus talked about in John 10:10.

If you're tired of feeling guilty about not sharing your faith, if you're tired of going month after month or year after year without knowing the joy of being used by the Holy Spirit to help someone come to Christ, if you're ready to be used by God in new and fresh ways, if you're ready to increase the days you remember on earth after you're in heaven—then read on! This book is for you!

IDENTIFY 1

Evangelism is not a professional job for a few trained men, but is instead the unrelenting responsibility of every person who belongs to the company of Jesus.

Elton Trueblood

I was experiencing every man's dream. Thanks to a friend who paid, I was sitting behind the wheel of a real NASCAR racing machine. There's nothing like going 100+ miles an hour around a genuine racing track (in this case, the Milwaukee Mile) in a car that was made to race. The tires, the suspension, the engine—every piece was designed to get this car around the track fast. The first lap or two I felt a bit nervous. The last thing I wanted to do was run this expensive car into a wall! Plus, it had a different feel to it than any other car I've ever driven. But as one lap turned into another, I felt more and more comfortable and any fear evaporated, leaving nothing but the sensation of outright thrill. "I'm actually driving a NASCAR car!" (And given my bent towards frugality, the added

13

thrill—"and I'm not paying for it!") It was an experience I will not soon forget.

It's like the story of when Jesus walked across the water on a midnight stroll (Matt. 14:22). At first the disciples were terrified. Jesus tried to calm their fears by telling them, "Hey guys, it's me." Peter wanted to test the theory. "Jesus if it's really you, let me come out on the water with you."

"Come on out," Jesus replied. Sure, Peter got a bit wet when he began to sink. But let's not forget, Peter is the only human in history who ever had the thrill of walking on water (that's something you'd always be able to tell your friends!).

Life with God was meant to be an adventure. Sure, there are plenty of ho-hum moments, but God did not create us with spiritual gifts and unique talents just so we would live a ho-hum life! We were born for a purpose. Let's go back to my day at the Milwaukee Mile. Some came to the track that day to do something I personally found a bit strange. They came and paid a handsome sum to sit in the passenger seat of a specially designed NASCAR vehicle and ride around the track with one of the staff drivers. Why in the world would you do that when you could actually drive the car?

14

This book is titled *5 Things Anyone Can Do to Introduce Others to Jesus*. Let's be honest, though. Statistics show we would just as soon sit in the passenger seat and forfeit the thrill of living the life God planned for us.

At first the experience of having spiritual conversations with others may be similar to how I felt behind the seat of that very expensive NASCAR vehicle. We're timid. We're afraid we're going to do something or say something that is going to bring the spiritual life of someone else into a terrific crash against the wall, never to be recovered.

When I first climbed into that car, after getting all the safety gear in place, I took a second and reminded myself that, yes, I *did* know how to drive a stick shift and yes, the accelerator and the brake were where they had always been. Reminding myself of those facts helped to calm my nervousness. When we join God in this adventure, we need to remind ourselves of some very important truths:

- 95 percent of all Christians have never won a soul to Christ.
- 80 percent of all Christians do not consistently engage in spiritual conversations with unchurched people.
- 96 percent of church leaders believe their churches would have grown faster if they would have been more involved in evangelism.

Source: Michael Parrott, "Street Level Evangelism," *Acts Evangelism* (1993), 9–11.

15

1. God is a good God and He would never call me to do something without giving me the power to do it. When Jesus gave us what has become known as The Great Commission (Matt. 28:18–20), He never intended it to cause us to break out into a cold sweat. When Peter asked Jesus if he could join Him out on the water, he already possessed power through the Holy Spirit. A few years later Peter experienced this exact same phenomenon when he stood up on the day of Pentecost and preached a powerful message that influenced thousands to come to Christ. Peter had untapped power inside him, placed there by God. In the same way, you have power living inside of you. How do I know this? Because God's character is such that He will not ask us to do something without giving us the power to do it. It may feel a bit intimidating at first, but when the power is needed, it will be there. Bank on it!

2. God was already drawing this person to himself long before I came into the picture. (See John 6:44.) There's a theological term for this; it's called prevenient grace. It's the strong pull of amazing grace that God uses to draw people to himself. Most of the time the unsaved person doesn't even realize it is happening (Rom. 5:8). God simply invites us to be part of this process of drawing people to

Him. We are not responsible for starting it, or bringing it to completion. All God asks of us is that we let Him work through us.

3. God cares infinitely more about this person coming to Him than I do; meaning He can make up for the honest mistakes I make. Many people are irrationally fearful they're going to say or do something that will cause someone to stop considering a life with Christ altogether. Sure, we may make a mistake along the way—but I have found that what people who are honestly seeking a relationship with Christ care about the most is my sincerity. If I can admit I don't know the answer to a question

> God is at work in the lives of those outside the church and invites us to join Him. He has created people with an incredible appetite for Him and He is actively at work in their lives drawing them to Himself.
>
> Ed Stetzer, *Breaking the Missional Code*

they're asking, or that I accidentally said something wrong, they'll be forgiving of that. They're not expecting me to be perfect, just honest.

WANTED: ADOPTION COORDINATOR

Sometimes when we're apprehensive what we need most is a good dose of motivation. Seeing other people climbing out of the NASCAR ahead of me grinning from ear to ear provided all the motivation I needed to climb in. My wife, Mary, and I have a friend named Bev. She's one of the most capable and gifted people we've ever met, and she is highly talented in her ability to make friends. For years she sold candles to supplement her income and she was great at it! I used to say Bev could sell candles to firemen in the middle of a blazing forest. When we planted Countryside Community Church in Spearfish, South Dakota, Bev was a critical member of a launch team that saw many people come into a relationship with Jesus Christ. Yet if Bev would have been born during the first century in the city of Ephesus, chances are she wouldn't have been allowed to live more than a few hours.

Bev was born with a deformed right arm. It extends no longer than her elbow. I've never seen it limit her in any way. She can do everything anyone with two fully func-tioning arms can do, but all that wouldn't have mattered. In first-century Ephesus, children born with birth defects of any kind were considered a "curse of the gods." A sign the gods were punishing the parents for something they had done in the past. Because no one wanted to keep around a constant reminder that they had upset the gods, their inclination was to "dismiss" this child as quickly as possible through euthanasia. Perhaps the gods would take pity on them and give them a "healthy" child next time. History tells us that just outside the city of Ephesus, near the bottom of a certain mountain, parents would take their newborn children who were deformed in any way and leave them there to die.

Occasionally people would walk up to the base of the mountain empty handed. Their goal was to find a baby they could bring home. Perhaps they were childless. Perhaps they felt the need for more help around the house. You know what this process of going to the mountain and saving a child who would have died otherwise was called? Adoption.

Keep this in mind as you read the opening words of Paul's letter to the people who lived in the city of Ephesus. "Even before he made the world, God loved us and chose us in Christ to be holy and *without fault* in his eyes. [His unchanging plan has always been] to *adopt us* into *his own family* by bringing us to himself through Jesus Christ . . . and it gave him *great pleasure*" (Eph. 1:4–5, emphasis mine).

Paul was saying we were the ones left on the mountain to die. Deformities caused by our own sin brought us there. But God in His mercy climbed the mountain to get us.

19

Jesus went to the cross (on another mountain) and paid the price for our sin. Now God looks right past those deformities. Through Christ He sees us as flawless. The Father's heart longs to adopt each one of us.

God's adoption process is ongoing. We are surrounded by so many who are still living with their spiritual, relational, and emotional deformities (sin), oblivious to the fact that God has already paid the price for their healing!

> I have called you back from the ends of the earth saying, "You are my servant." For I have chosen you and will not throw you away.
>
> Isaiah 41:9

So what is the responsibility of those who have already experienced adoption by the Father? Are we to sit and become comfortable while others are left to die? Absolutely not! God calls us to join Him in the adoption process.

As it turns out, I'm writing this chapter in Ukraine. My wife and I are here adopting two beautiful children through the help of a Ukrainian translator/facilitator. Our friend has translated countless official documents from English to Ukrainian and has helped with everything the government requires for our adoption to be successful.

In a very real sense, you and I are called to be adoption facilitators. We are not the principle players in this process. God is the one seeking His children. He loves them more than we could ever imagine. But for reasons we will probably not fully understand until we get to heaven, He has chosen to express His love to others *through us*! We are the translators of God's love to our friends, family members, coworkers, neighbors, even acquaintances such as the barista at the local Starbucks, or the person who cuts our hair. These are the people God wants to adopt into His family. And He's calling us to join Him as "adoption facilitators."

One of the children we are adopting is four years old. Because my wife and I don't speak any Ukrainian, this makes the language barrier a bit "interesting" to say the least. We want to tell our new children we love them, but telling them in English means absolutely nothing to them. So, thanks to our translator, we've learned how to say it in Ukrainian. Do we say the words exactly right? Probably not. But we're rewarded with a big smile when we say it. In the same way, God uses us to help explain to others His amazing love for them.

21

Chances are, right now, there are people in your life God wants to speak to through you! People He has put in your "orbit" simply because He knows that if you will be obedient and represent Him to these "adoption candidates" they will experience New Life! It may not happen through one conversation—it rarely does. Forgive me for using one more illustration about adopting, but it fits. Four-year-olds don't automatically trust us when we meet them—it takes time. When it comes to spiritual matters, we don't automatically gain the trust of someone who is not in a relationship with God overnight. It can take weeks, months, even years. But like anything great in life, the outcome is worth the effort!

IDENTIFYING INTEREST

So how do I specifically identify the people God wants to reach through me?

Not long ago, Rick Warren wrote an article for his Web site (www.pastors.com) entitled "How to Recognize Spiritual Receptivity in Your Community." In it, Rick mentions two groups of people who tend to be most open to spiritual matters: (1) People in transition. These are people experiencing significant change, either positive or negative. (2) People under tension. He writes: "God uses all kinds of emotional pain to get people's attention: the pain of divorce, death of a loved one, unemployment, financial problems, marriage and family difficulties, loneliness, resentment, guilt, and other stresses."

What I have found best is to simply pray a prayer like this: *Holy Spirit, I am available to be used as you wish to bring others to Christ. Help me to see the people I come in contact with today through your eyes.*

Have you ever had the experience of buying a new car (or a car that's new to you)? Before you bought it, you hardly saw that car model around town, but once you bought it, you saw cars just like it everywhere. Your eyes were "tuned" to see it. In the same way, if we will petition God, He will give us eyes to see people in a whole new light—the way He sees them. When that happens, *everything* changes.

Do you know the story of Samuel being sent to anoint the next king of Israel? The Chris Conrad paraphrase goes something like this: "Sam, I want you to go down to Bethlehem because the person I've chosen to be the next king lives there. He's one of the sons of a man named Jesse. When you get there, I'll show you which person to anoint." When Samuel arrived in Bethlehem and met Jesse's oldest son, he was convinced this must be the one

23

God had chosen. This is what the Bible actually says: "Samuel took one look at Eliab and thought, 'Surely this is the LORD's anointed!' But the LORD said to Samuel, 'Don't judge by his appearance or height . . . The LORD doesn't see things the way you see things. People judge by outward appearance, but the LORD looks at the heart" (1 Sam. 16:6–7).

I remember one night I took our dog for a walk to the top of Signal Hill . . . In that night I heard the city, and God's voice spoke to my heart. I heard wives and husbands screaming at each other. I heard dogs barking, cars screeching, sirens blaring, and guns shooting. I heard the things that Jesus hears when He listens to the city, and I began to weep. In that moment, the Lord broke my heart for the city and the people of the city enslaved to darkness.

Neil Cole, *Organic Church*

We often can't tell just by looking if God has brought someone to the point where they're open to spiritual things. But God in His faithfulness will reveal that to us. Our responsibility is to pray that He'll make it clear—He'll take care of the rest.

Remember, God's already given you the power. The only question remaining is will you join God in the adventure He has set before you?

KEY POINTS

- Life with God was meant to be an adventure.
- That adventure includes joining Him in introducing people to Jesus Christ.
- God has already given us the power to do what He's called us to do.
- God wants to enlist us as "adoption facilitators" for Him.
- The people who tend to be most open to the gospel are those who are "In Transition" or "Under Tension."

DISCUSSION QUESTIONS

1. Can you think of someone in your life that is truly living the Christian life as an adventure? If so, who?

2. Was there anyone who was influential in you becoming a Christian? If so, who?

3. Why do you think 95 percent of Christians have never won anyone to Jesus Christ?

4. Has God begun to place on your heart and mind someone for whom He may want you to be an "adoption facilitator"? Who?

ACTION STEPS

IDENTIFY

1. Make a list of about five people you know who appear to be most open to the gospel.

2. Ask God to remove any callousness that may have crept into your heart towards people who do not know Him.

3. Ask God to open your eyes and break your heart for the people around you who are doing life without Him.

4. Be sensitive to the "divine appointments" God gives you with unsaved people. These are spiritual conversations that seem to come out of nowhere but are actually strategically planned by God for the benefit of the unsaved person.

RESOURCES

- Neil Cole—*The Organic Church*
- Ed Stetzer—*Breaking the Missional Code*
- Bill Hybels and Mark Mittleberg—*Becoming a Contagious Christian*
- Bill Hybels—*A Walk Across the Room*

INTERCEDE 2

*In no other way can the believer become as fully
involved with God's work, especially the work of
world evangelism, as in intercessory prayer.*

Dick Eastman, president of Every Home for Christ

My father is Mr. Fix It! He can fix anything around the
house. Me? Not so much. The other day we had a small
household fan break. I looked at it, sized up the problem
and realized I had one of three options: (1) throw it away
and buy a new one; (2) spend hours trying to fix it and be
utterly frustrated through the whole process; or (3) put it
in a box, ship it to my dad, and let Mr. Fix It do it!

I chose option 3. Within minutes of receiving my broken
fan in the mail, he had the thing working again beautifully
and was ready to take it back to the post office. As far as
I was concerned, it was a win-win situation. My father,
who is retired, got a "fix it" project he could work on,
which he loves, and I got saved from what certainly would
have been hours of sheer frustration.

The difference between my father and me is not only that he is much more naturally talented toward fixing things, it is that he also has all the right tools to fix everything. I have one medium sized toolbox. It's got some screwdrivers, a hammer, a few different types of pliers, etc. My father has an entire area of his basement reserved for his tools. At one time or another he has bought, used, given away or eventually worn out every Craftsman tool Sears sells.

I've never known him to go to Sears to buy a tool just to say he's got one of those lying around "just in case." Over the last fifty-five years of his adult life, he has purchased tools that he needed to complete a specific job. He knew that his skills, plus the right tool, could solve 99 percent of the problems that came up around the house.

Whether you're a "fix it" guy like my dad or more on my side of the spectrum, I think we've all had experiences when we felt if we just had the right "tool," whatever we were trying to do would be so much easier.

I shared with you in chapter 1 that this book is being written while in Ukraine. While I've been here, I've learned this "right tool" lesson in both the negative and positive form. The little apartment we're staying in has no oven and no microwave, just a cooktop stove. My wife is cooking some *amazing* meals—but I speak for both of us when I say we're missing our microwave at home. Many times, the microwave is "just the right tool" to make our lives a little easier.

On the positive side, I'm using a laptop computer that my company provides to write this book and work on other projects while I'm here. Being able to take my work with me via a laptop makes a *tremendous* difference in my productivity. One thing's for sure, when we have just the right tool (whatever it is), our lives are so much smoother and easier, and many times we don't have to expend near as much energy.

I grew up in Southern California but have spent the last sixteen years of my life in snow country. For the first twelve years I dealt with snow the old fashioned way . . . I shoveled it. It was a great way to get exercise in the middle of the winter. Most of my neighbors had snow blowers, which meant what took me an hour and left me soaking wet with sweat took them ten minutes (with no need for a shower when they were done). Eventually, my parents, who felt sorry for me, bought me a snow blower. Interestingly enough, I still spend the same amount of

29

time outside as I used to, the difference is now, once I'm done snow-blowing my own driveway and sidewalk, I go to houses on my street where people do not have snow blowers and help them clear their driveways.

Here's what I've noticed about many Christians, myself included. We have been given the best tool available in the universe to help other people, but all too often we allow it to gather dust and even begin to rust in the garage of our spiritual life. I've sometimes called this tool the "secret weapon of the Christian life." I refer to it as a secret weapon because it has nuclear-sized power. As a Christ-follower, you are armed and dangerous!

Before we unveil what it is, let's take just a moment and talk about what it's *not*:

(1) Our full knowledge about all truth (i.e. our ability to answer *every* question a person might ask us about Christianity). Yes, it is important for us to know as much as we can about our faith (1 Pet. 3:15), but our knowledge alone is not enough to break through a person's spiritual defenses.

(2) The lack of a dynamic testimony. Many people believe what hinders their ability to be more effective in talking to their friends, neighbors, coworkers, and acquaintances about their faith in Jesus Christ is the fact that they don't have a "dynamic" testimony. God will bring people into your life that need to hear exactly what *you* have to share.

(3) A particular personality trait. Some people assume if they're not super outgoing or lack the spiritual gift of evangelism (Eph. 4:11), they will never be successful in sharing their faith. That's not true either. You can absolutely be effective in helping people come into a relationship with Christ if you use the secret weapon effectively.

So what is it? This secret weapon? Intercessory prayer.

Intercessory prayer, as we will see, is a specific type of prayer that unleashes the power of heaven in intentional and strategic ways.

DOES PRAYER REALLY CHANGE THINGS?

Intercessory prayer makes all the difference! It is how we tap into God's all-encompassing power and aim it at specific "targets." The great news is that we don't have to be a

31

monk or a nun to practice intercessory prayer. We can be people who live in a fast-paced society and have many responsibilities and still enjoy the benefits this type of prayer produces.

What is intercession? Webster defines *intercession* as the ability "to go or pass between; to act between parties with a view to reconcile those who differ or contend."

Intercessory prayer is simply the process of placing ourselves between God and our friends and asking God to release His power so that they will be drawn to a relationship with Jesus Christ.

For reasons we will probably not understand until we experience heaven, God often chooses to limit His power to the things we pray for. The issue is not *can* God do things without our prayer—of course He can. He set the whole world in motion through creation without any involvement on our part. He is omnipotent, supreme in His power. But for some reason He has chosen to limit to what degree that power is released here on earth based on our prayers.

32

In case you need a little more convincing of this, let me remind you of a story. God promised Abraham that one day He would give Abraham's decedents the land eventually referred to as "The Promised Land."

"Yes, I will give the entire land of Canaan . . . to you and to your descendants . . . and I will be their God" (Gen. 17:8). That was a clear promise of God, a promise that could not be broken.

God repeated this promise to Abraham's grandson, Jacob, in Genesis 46:2–4:

> During the night God spoke to [Jacob] in a vision. "Jacob! Jacob!" he called. "Here I am," Jacob replied. "I am God, the God of your father," the voice said. "Do not be afraid to go down to Egypt, for there I will make your family into a great nation. I will go with you down to Egypt, and I will bring you back again. But you will die in Egypt with Joseph attending to you."

So, God had already promised to bring His people back to Canaan from Egypt, but what prompted the Exodus to actually begin to unfold? The Bible tells us that within God's calling of Moses:

> Then the LORD told him, "I have certainly seen the oppression of my people in Egypt. I have heard their cries of distress because of their harsh slave drivers. Yes, I am aware of their suffering. So I have come down to rescue them from the power of the Egyptians and lead them out of Egypt into their own fertile and spacious land. It is a land flowing with milk and honey . . . (Ex. 3:7–8)

It was the cries of God's people for deliverance that moved God's hand in power. There are other examples in the Bible of God limiting what He does on earth to what we pray for (Ezek. 22:30–31; 2 Chron. 7:14).

> Even though God's existence and character are completely independent of any created thing (see Acts 17:24, 25) and God already has all resources in His hands (see Job 41:11; Psalm 50:10–12), God needs our prayers.
>
> Dutch Sheets, *Intercessory Prayer*

Are you beginning to understand why I call it our secret weapon? What all this means is that your prayers matter! And they matter a lot!

A few years ago, Henry Blackaby cowrote a workbook called *Experiencing God* that was widely circulated and used in the church. One of the enduring principles I took from going through that book with my church board was, "Stop asking God to bless what you're doing and start getting involved with what God is already blessing."

If we pray prayers that we know are already in accordance to His will, then we can experience maximum prayer effectiveness. We already know God has a heart for people outside a relationship with Him. He had a heart for us when we were doing life without Him and He has that same heart for others. We know His heart aches for them to come into a relationship with Him. We also know

> We must understand that our sovereign God has for His own reasons so designed this world that much of what is truly His will He makes contingent on the attitudes and the actions of human beings. He allows humans to make decisions that can influence history . . . Human inaction does not nullify the atonement, but human inaction can make the atonement ineffective for lost people.
>
> C. Peter Wagner,
> *Confronting the Powers*

from the life of Jesus that God will do just about anything (except go against His character) to bring people back to himself. He allowed His son to be crucified for our sins— there's no greater price He could have paid.

35

So when you and I begin to pray for the people around us to come into a relationship with God, we can know these prayers are lined up within His will and are dripping with potential.

INITIALIZING INTERCESSION

Now let's turn our attention to what specifically we should be praying for.

Pray that they'll be receptive. Jesus told a parable which has become known as "The Parable of the Sower" in Matthew 13. In that story, Jesus made it clear that there are different responses to the gospel message. We start out by praying that God would cause the hearts of our friends to become softened so they will be receptive to God's love for them personally.

This often puts us in a bit of an interesting dilemma. We love our friends and we wouldn't wish any harm to them; still, we want them to come into a relationship with Jesus Christ, which often doesn't happen if they are totally content. Often I find myself praying to God, "Lord, allow them to feel a sense of emptiness in their life that draws them to you."

36

What we're ultimately praying here is that God would begin to soften their hearts toward Him. That their spiritually blinded eyes would begin to be open to the fact that God does exist, that He is longing to be in a relationship with them, and that a life with God is by far the best life to live.

Pray that they'll be released. In this same parable of the sower, Jesus described a very real enemy who is not interested in our friends becoming followers of Jesus Christ (Matt. 13:9). Because of that, he does everything he can to "snatch" away the awesome news about the forgiveness, grace, and life we find in Jesus Christ from individuals who are honestly seeking truth about spiritual things. Therefore, we need to pray that our friends will be released from any control the enemy may have on them.

For those of you sci-fi fanatics out there, think of it like a force field. The enemy has our friends under his control and he's not interested in giving it up. But through intercessory prayer, we can pinpoint the power of God onto the hold the enemy has on them and break the control.

My brother is a rocket scientist. Most of what he works on is considered "top secret" so I really have no idea what he does. However, I do remember vividly a conversation I had with him fifteen years ago when we were talking about the accuracy of intercontinental missiles. I asked him about what the range of acceptable parameters were, i.e., if for some strange reason a missile were aimed at our house, would hitting the neighbor's house be considered a success because at least you were close? I'll never forget his answer (which he wouldn't have been able to give me if it was classified). "If the bomb was aimed at the living room of this house and it hit the kitchen instead, it would be considered a failure." If man-made missiles that travel halfway around the world are that accurate, imagine the accuracy of the response of God, who is ever present with us, to our prayers.

When you were a kid, did you ever play with a magnifying glass, catching the sun and shooting it towards the ground? Do you remember the sense that the power of the sun was being directed, pinpointed to a specific point on the concrete?

That's the kind of powerful accuracy our prayers can have when we pray against the enemy by prayers such as: "In the powerful name of Jesus Christ I break any control you have on (the person's name) life. I command you to give up that control through the resurrection power of Jesus."

This may be a new style of praying for you. It doesn't have to be weird. You don't have to pray this out loud if you're uncomfortable doing that. Just pray this in your heart. Better yet, pray it out loud in your car when you're driving down the freeway. Because Satan is not interested in giving up his control, this is the kind of prayer you may need to pray over a period of time, not just once. Both in Daniel (10:10–14) and in Luke (18:1–8), the Bible encourages us to pray about something until we see results.

Pray that they'll be responsive. It's one thing to feel like you should make a change; it's another thing to actually make that change. There were many times when I felt like I should lose weight and go on a diet, but it was a different thing all together when I woke up one day and said, "I'm changing my eating habits." (That was eight years ago; I lost nearly one hundred pounds and have kept it off thanks to God's help.)

39

There are times when our non-Christian friends will want to change, feel the need to change, but not actually do what's necessary to change. During this time in our friends' lives, we can play a powerful role through our prayers, asking God to give them the determination they need to draw a line in the sand, cross over to faith, and make a lasting change.

Paul, in his second letter to the Corinthians, does a really great job summing up our prayer for our friends: "As God's partners, we beg you not to accept this marvelous gift of God's kindness and then ignore it. For God says, 'At just the right time, I heard you. On the day of salvation, I helped you.' Indeed, the 'right time' is now. Today is the day of salvation" (2 Cor. 6:1–2).

To sum it up, we need to pray that our friends will actually hear the Good News and be responsive to His offer of forgiveness and a new life.

I love how Luke begins chapter 18 of the book that bears his name. "Jesus told them a story showing that it was necessary for them to pray consistently and never quit" (Luke 18:1 MSG). During this process of praying for your friends, you might be tempted to give up when you don't see immediate results. Don't let this happen to you! Your persistence in this process can make all the difference in the world.

You have just the right tool.

You have a secret weapon at your disposal.

For the sake of someone who is out of a relationship with Christ, who's life can be powerfully changed by your intercessory prayer. I implore you. *Use it!*

KEY POINTS

- Christians have at their disposal a secret weapon.
- That secret weapon is the power of intercessory prayer.
- Pray that they'll be *receptive*.
- Pray that they'll be *released*.
- Pray that they'll be *responsive*.

DISCUSSION QUESTIONS

1. Prior to you opening up your heart to Jesus Christ, was there anyone you know of who was praying for you to become a Christian?

2. Have you ever witnessed firsthand the power of prayer and the difference it can make?

3. Do you see any specific things your non-Christian friends need to be released from?

4. What is a "reminder trigger" you can use to remember to pray for them on a daily basis?

ACTION STEPS

1. Commit to pray daily for the non-Christian friends God has laid on your heart.

2. Make yourself a "trigger" reminder such as the clock in your car or another object you see daily to remind you to pray.

3. Pray that their hearts would begin to soften toward God.

4. Pray that they will be receptive, released, and responsive.

5. Pray specifically that they will open up their hearts and begin a relationship with Jesus Christ.

RESOURCES

- C. Peter Wagner—*Prayer Shield*
- Dutch Sheets—*Intercessory Prayer*
- Becky Tirabassi—*Let Prayer Change Your Life*
- Mark Moore—*The Rhythm of Prayer*
- Keith Drury—*There Is No I in Church*

INTERSECT 3

*All souls are equally precious but not
all are equally strategic.*

Dr. Joe Aldrich, *Lifestyle Evangelism*

Imagine the life of a caterpillar. No, not the big yellow kind
that moves massive amounts of dirt—the kind with all the
tiny legs. What if a caterpillar had enough self-awareness
to know what his life was going to be like? "For a while
I'm going to live like this, walking everywhere, munching
on leaves and trying to keep safe from birds who would
love to have me for lunch. But eventually I'm going to spin
myself a cocoon where I'm going to live while God
produces an incredible metamorphosis in my body. When
it's over, I'll bust out of that cocoon a beautiful butterfly no
longer subjected to walking. I'll have wings! I'll be able to
fly everywhere I want to go."

Now imagine you're a caterpillar that got stuck in the
cocoon stage. You wove your cocoon, God worked His

45

miracle of metamorphosis in your life, but you chose to stay in your cocoon. You got comfortable. Too comfortable.

How about it? Would you choose to live in a cocoon, confined to a very small place? For those of you with claustrophobia, just reading that makes you nervous. And yet, as amazing as it sounds, that's how a vast majority of so-called "committed Christians" choose to live their lives.

The leadership of a sister denomination was asked about the time they give to people outside the "Christian cocoon." This is what they said:

- 49 percent said they spend zero time in an average week ministering outside of the church.
- 89 percent said they have zero time reserved on their list of weekly priorities for "going out to evangelize."

Source: Michael Parrott, "Street Level Evangelism," *Acts Evangelism* (1993), 9–11.

Let me explain what I mean. Prior to becoming a Christian, we were in our caterpillar stage. We were walking around seeing life from underneath. Then God blessed us with His incredible mercy. Through the work of Jesus Christ, we are transformed from the inside out (2 Cor. 5:17). But then we do something very strange. We begin to walk away from our non-Christian friends. Usually new Christians don't even realize they are doing this. They see in front of them a loving new community of new friends at church, who all seem to care about them and want to encourage them. Hence they start spending a vast majority of time with their new friends. Study people's lives six months or a year after they've become a Christian and what you'll find is that a vast majority of them will have abandoned all their non-Christian friends to live in a "Christian cocoon." This is not the life the Father intended for us.

We were created by God, reconciled to Him by the work of Jesus Christ, and commissioned (Matt. 28) to join Him in this grand adventure of seeing other people come to Him. Yet way too many Christ-followers get comfortable in a Christian subculture and stay there, their senses slowly becoming dull toward a massive sea of people around them who do not know the forgiveness, peace, and abundant life Jesus came to give.

A cocoon is not where we belong! We are to be in the world, just not corrupted by it. (See John 17:13.) Paul makes this clear in 2 Corinthians 5:

> This means that anyone who belongs to Christ has
> become a new person. The old life is gone; a new
> life has begun! And all of this is a gift from God,
> who brought us back to himself through Christ.

47

And *God has given us this task of reconciling people to him.* For God was in Christ, reconciling the world to himself, no longer counting people's sins against them. And he gave us this wonderful message of reconciliation. *So we are Christ's ambassadors* . . . (2 Cor. 5:17–20, emphasis mine)

You and I are "Christ's ambassadors." Will you allow me to ask an obvious question? Where does an ambassador live most of the time? An ambassador has continual contact with their home country through phone conversations, e-mails, letters, etc., but their primary responsibilities take place in representing their home country within a foreign one.

As Christ's ambassadors, we are to have continual contact with our "home country" through church, small groups, personal prayer and Bible Study, etc. But in order to be an ambassador, our focus must be on the outside world, those who have yet to come into a relationship with Christ.

WON'T THIS FEEL FAKE?

48   Aren't you glad we no longer live in the day of arranged marriages? Whether you are single or married, a common thread we enjoy about relationships is the privilege of

being able to choose who we date and ultimately who we marry, if marriage is to be part of God's plan for our lives.

The same is true in friendships. We choose our friends. In a technological age, where so many people interact with a computer or other machines all day, friendships are held as prized possessions.

It's this very fact that causes some people to never talk to other people about their relationship with Jesus Christ. When the subject is brought up they get an uneasy feeling. A distress that can be summed up this way: "I do not feel comfortable building a relationship with someone just so they can be a target of my evangelistic efforts. It feels totally unauthentic to me; like I'm doing a bait and switch on them." Often the people who are gifted by God to make and keep wonderful friendships with people that could lead into that person becoming a Christian never develop those friendships because they are so afraid of being considered a fraud by the very person they would be sharing with.

Is there a solution? Absolutely! And it's not complicated.

Ultimately it all comes down to our motives. What is driving us to build these relationships? All too often a Christ-follower will hear a message about witnessing and feel guilty about their lack of involvement in helping others meet Jesus. They start thinking about their non-Christian friends. They leave church that day with this internal conflict going on, a conflict I've never heard anyone really talk about. It's the conflict between a genuine desire for your friends to become Christians and the fear that they will think the only reason you now care about them is so you can talk to them about spiritual things.

This is a conflict we never see displayed by the people in the New Testament. Why?

It goes back to a conversation Jesus had with one of the religious experts of His day. An expert in religious law tried to trap him with this question: "'Teacher, which is the most important commandment in the law of Moses?' Jesus replied, 'You must love the LORD your God with all your heart, all your soul, and all your mind.' This is the first and greatest commandment. A second is equally important: 'Love your neighbor as yourself'" (Matt. 22:35–39).

50   It's that straightforward. Love God wholeheartedly. Love your neighbor.

If we come at this subject from a position of guilt, "I should share my faith with my friends; it's my responsibility to do this; God is expecting me to do it so I have to," then the focus is on our duty to accomplish a task. Our friends just become "pawns" in the whole process. It feels like an arranged marriage, like a contractual obligation. No wonder there is a conflict in our hearts!

Jesus never intended for the Great Commission (to be witnesses for Him) to be separated from the Great Commandment (to love others deeply). If we have truly fallen in love with Jesus and are overwhelmed with all He has done for us, and if we have truly allowed Him to give us His love for our non-Christian friends, then the conflict inside of us disappears. Non-Christians are no longer "projects" or our "witnessing responsibility." They are people for us to genuinely love and care for. People made in the image of God who are not experiencing the joy and forgiveness that comes from being in a relationship with Him.

ALL IN GOOD TIME

There's another factor we haven't mentioned yet that can also cause us to feel fake. It's the issue of timing. After hearing a message on witnessing, people feel the need to "win their non-Christian friends to Jesus" immediately. "After all," they reason, "my friends could get hit by a Mack truck tomorrow and then I'll be left with the guilt that I never shared Jesus with them!" (Notice again how the motive behind all this is to appease our potential guilt.)

What God is asking of us is that we move in rhythm with Him and the work He is already doing in our friends' lives. For nearly all my life, I have gone to a hair stylist (as opposed to a barber). Don't ask me why, I certainly don't have spectacular hair to style. It must be because my parents took me to the same hair stylist who cut my dad's hair. Over the years, I have come to realize that my monthly hair appointments can be dynamic opportunities to join God in His reaching toward people who don't know Him. As a result I've seen several of them come to Christ.

Sharing Christ's love with your hair stylist is an interesting dynamic because you only see them once a month, or so, and then only for forty-five minutes. Still, I have made it a habit to pray before each appointment and ask God to guide the conversation in a way that will build confidence and trust and pave the way for me to eventually talk to them about their need for Christ. In other words, I have an "I'm in this for the long haul" mindset with them.

About eight months ago, I moved to a new city and with the move came the opportunity to find a new hair stylist. Over the last eight months, I have been slowly building a rapport with her. Slowly but surely, I could tell trust was beginning to build. During my latest appointment, she was telling me about an area of her life that was causing her a great deal of frustration and disappointment. I felt the Holy Spirit prompting me and so I simply said to her, "You know, I really think what's going on in your life is that your soul is crying out for a relationship with God and you're trying to fill that need with a lot of other things that were never designed to fill it." She looked right at me and said, "I think you're right."

My assumption is that the Holy Spirit will prompt me to continue our spiritual conversation next month, we'll see. My point is this. It's taken eight months to get us to the point where we could talk about her spiritual life. Does it always take this long? No. But the length of time doesn't matter. My responsibility is to be obedient to the prompt-ings of the Holy Spirit, whenever they come. If He would have prompted me to say something on my first visit to her salon chair, I would have done it. But He didn't. His timing is always perfect, I just need to trust it and move with Him.

Prior to the move, we lived in the same town for six years and for all those years I went to the same hair stylist. I remember several times getting very frustrated, because my monthly time with this person didn't appear to be going anywhere. I remember praying and saying, "Holy Spirit, are you sure you don't want me to go somewhere else?" But each time I sensed Him say, "Stay put." One afternoon, I got a call from her. It's not very often that your hair stylist calls you out of the blue. She asked me if I would be open to doing some marriage counseling with her and her husband. This eventually opened up the door to some wonderful opportunities to share my faith. She began to attend our church. After a Sunday morning service, she shared with me that she had accepted the Lord. I remember driving home from church that day saying, "God, help me always to stay on the same page with you and not to give up when you're just getting ready to do something really cool in a person's life."

There will be times when we are amazed at how quickly we find ourselves in a significant spiritual conversation with someone. There'll be other times when we wonder why it's not going more quickly. But it's not our responsibility to "sell" something. It's our responsibility to be an "adoption facilitator" and follow promptings of the Holy Spirit, whenever they come.

The final key point is to intersect the lives of our non-Christian friends in a way that is comfortable for them. The apostle Paul was a master at this. Take a minute and read this passage:

I try to find common ground with everyone, doing everything I can to save some. I do everything to spread the Good News and share in its blessings. Don't you realize that in a race everyone runs, but only one person gets the prize? So run to win! All athletes are disciplined in their training. They do it to win a prize that will fade away, but we do it for an eternal prize. So I run with purpose in every step. I am not just shadowboxing. I discipline my body like an athlete, training it to do what it should. Otherwise, I fear that after preaching to others I myself might be disqualified. (1 Cor. 9:22–27)

55

When Paul penned these words concerning purpose, he was specifically talking about his strategic thinking toward being a witness for Christ. Paul was very determined to not let anything get in his way of introducing people to Jesus. So what did He do? He "tried to find common ground."

I've lost track of how many things I've done in the name of building "common ground." From kayaking to working on cars to eating food I normally wouldn't enjoy. But in the end the friendships that have been forged and the bridges that have been built have been well worth it.

When can we find time to do this? We're all running from here to there trying to keep up with the demands that pull on us. One of the benefits of being a disciple of Jesus is that we can study His life closely. And when we do, we see that He never appeared to be in a rush.

Look at His words in Matthew 11 from *The Message* paraphrase: "Walk with me and work with me—watch how I do it. Learn the unforced rhythms of grace. I won't lay anything heavy or ill-fitting on you. Keep company with me and you'll learn to live freely and lightly" (Matt. 11:29–30 MSG).

In our hurried world, Jesus encourages us to slow down and to join Him in the work He is already doing in other people's lives. Instead of driving right past our neighbor's house, slow down and get to know them . . . today! Instead of just always walking by your coworkers' cubicles, take a minute to stop and invite them to lunch or get to know them over a coffee break. Yes, we all have schedules—but that's just it, we have schedules. God has purpose for our lives. He wants our lives to matter. I'd rather be in sync with His purpose than my schedule anytime. But this means there are going to be times when my schedule is going to be interrupted because He wants to accomplish His purpose through me. This means we might be late to something or we might have to skip a workout or an afternoon off we were looking forward to because God asks us to help or just "hang out" with someone who is presently far from Him. But in the end, we'll be so glad we did.

Look for opportunities today and this week to intersect the lives of a non-Christian friends around you. And remember, they are not your "project." They are people to be loved. Your love for God and your love for them will lead you to the right results.

- As Christians we are called to be ambassadors for Christ, which means we are not to live in a Christian cocoon.

- Guilt is the wrong motivation for being a witness. This just leads to building relationships that are fake and superficial.

- The correct motivation for being a witness is a genuine response to the Great Commission in the spirit of the Great Commandment. This leads to a genuine love for others and an ongoing commitment to them, regardless of how quickly they are receptive to spiritual conversations.

- God's timing is perfect. We often get discouraged that our friendships are not producing instant results. As we follow the Holy Spirit's promptings, He will guide us as to when to talk to our friends about Christ. It may be the first day we meet them, it may be months afterwards.

- Only if we are willing to slow down will we find the time to spend with the non-Christian people in our lives God is calling us to love and befriend.

DISCUSSION QUESTIONS

1. Was there someone who left the "Christian cocoon" and reached out to you, showing interest in your life and influencing you to become a Christian? If so, who was this person and what kinds of things did they do?

2. What do you think it looks like for you to be an ambassador for Christ? Would you say you are spending adequate time in the "world" of the non-Christians in your life?

3. Can you say with integrity that it is love for your non-Christian friends that is motivating you to be a quality ambassador and not your own sense of guilt?

4. Do you need to turn off the radio or the TV long enough to hear the Holy Spirit's voice as He prompts you to adjust your schedule so you can be in sync with His plans for your day?

ACTION STEPS

1. If you don't know, ask your friends what their hobbies are or what they enjoy doing on their days off.

2. See if you can find some common interests. The range of this is limitless—from fantasy football leagues to Rotary Clubs to exercise classes to cooking together to fixing up old cars.

3. Spend plenty of time on "their turf" building levels of trust.

4. Listen to the Holy Spirit's voice as He leads you toward having a spiritual conversation with your friends.

RESOURCES

- Scott Dawson—*The Complete Evangelism Guidebook: Expert Advice on Reaching Others for Christ*
- Will McRaney—*The Art of Personal Evangelism: Sharing Jesus in a Changing Culture*

INVITE 4

How shall I feel at the judgement, if multitudes of missed opportunities pass before me in full review, and all my excuses prove to be disguises of my cowardice and pride.

Dr. W. E. Sangster

During my senior year in college, I started dating the beautiful woman who would eventually become my wife. After years of knowing her, a good solid dating period, asking the council of some wise people around me and praying for wisdom and discernment, I came to the point where I knew it was time to ask her to marry me. I asked her on a beach in Santa Barbara, California, and fortunately for me she said yes. My life has been forever enriched.

Chances are you've known people who were dating someone and they seemed right for each other, it's just the guy was too afraid to pop the question, so the couple sat in relational limbo-land for months, if not years. Eventually girls get tired of this, and understandably

61

so. If we truly love someone, that love "expels all fear" (1 John 4:18) and should compel us into action.

The exact same principle holds true in our relationships with non-Christians. All too often when it comes to spiritual conversations, we focus on our fear and not on their need to hear about God's love for them. Instead of being proactive and continually looking for Holy-Spirit-inspired opportunities to talk to them about a relationship with Christ, we bury our heads in the sand and pretend it's somebody else's responsibility (our pastor's, someone who knows more theological facts than we do, someone with the spiritual gift of evangelism, someone more outgoing than us, etc.). When it gets right down to it, an honest assessment of the situation would conclude that we're more concerned with our comfort than with loving them enough to start a spiritual conversation.

By now our friends know us and trust us well enough that not to talk to them about our relationship with God would be to hide something that's very significant in our lives. The need now is for us to explain our faith in easy to understand language. Depending on how much time has passed from the days when you lived without Christ, you might be tempted to think, "They probably already know what I believe; I don't need to say anything." Nothing could be further from the truth!

Your friends might be aware by now of your spiritual activity (you go to church) but they have no clear understanding of what motivates you to do that. They assume we ascribe to a "religion." They have no comprehension of the awesome relationship that is available to them. There is so much they

- About one-third of born agains (33 percent) believe that if a person is good enough they can earn a place in heaven (2005).
- 28 percent of born agains agree that "while He lived on earth, Jesus committed sins, like other people," compared to 42 percent of all adults (2005).

don't know that some very simple, straightforward conversations about spiritual things could enlighten them about.

LOCKER-ROOM PEP TALK

Team, I want to congratulate you. You have worked hard. You have **identified** people outside a relationship with Christ; you have begun to **intercede** for them, asking God that your friends would be receptive, released and responsive; you've taken time to **intersect** their lives. That's awesome! Way to go! Now continually look for the opportunity to "make a play" out there on the field called

63

real life. Look for opportunities to respond to the Holy Spirit promptings He will give you to say something for Him. And while you're out there, here are some very important things to remember:

(1) Those who have spiritual conversations, who involve themselves with God's harvesting process are promised "good wages" and "joy" (John 4:36). We serve a God who has all the resources of the universe available to Him, so when He says that He pays "good wages," that's something to take note of!

(2) Another important lesson that comes to us out of John 4:35–38 is that there is joy for the planter *and* the harvester both. There are going to be times when the Holy Spirit prompts me to have a spiritual conversation with someone and, although it is a good conversation, the person indicates they are still not ready to "cross over the line" and begin a relationship with Christ. Too many people are tempted to walk away from that kind of conversation feeling like they failed. They didn't fail at all! They were very successful at planting seeds.

64

There will be several of these conversations prior to someone opening up their heart to Jesus Christ. Maybe I was the first in a series of seven. Maybe I was number five. Sometimes I have the privilege of being number seven and seeing the person come to Christ right there in a restaurant or on a golf course or in Starbucks. The point is, celebrate each part of this process . . . God does! And besides, being a "planter" in this process is much more rewarding than sitting and staring at the field or the crop and never doing anything about it.

(3) While our ultimate prayer and goal is that our friends would begin a relationship with Christ, their salvation is not our responsibility. The responsibility of salvation lies directly in the nail-pierced hands of our Savior. Our responsibility is to be faithful to the promptings the Holy Spirit gives us to share. On a football team, one individual is not responsible for everything that happens on a field. It takes a team to win a game. In the same way, we need to realize that what God holds us responsible for is playing the part He asks us to play. If we are obedient to Him and have a spiritual conversation with someone (or a series of spiritual conversations) and the person never responds, God does not hold us responsible for the lack of response.

65

(4) Jesus promised us power! You're probably familiar with Acts 1:8 where Jesus says, "But you will receive

power when the Holy Spirit comes upon you. And you will be my witnesses, telling people about me everywhere . . ."

Notice, Jesus doesn't promise His power will be made available for us to do just anything we want to do. He's promising His power is going to be uniquely channeled toward one of the most important aspects of the kingdom, telling people about Him.

We're not doing this in our power but in His!

We're simply joining God in what He's already doing in a person's life. Have you ever read the story of Philip and the Ethiopian eunuch in Acts 8:26–40? What about the story of Peter and Cornelius in Acts 10? If you haven't read these stories in a while, can I encourage you to put this book down and take the next fifteen minutes and read those two stories?

What we see displayed in both of these stories is that God was already at work long before Philip or Peter came on the scene. They did not get the spiritual ball rolling—and this same pattern is displayed throughout the book of Acts. God prompts, His people follow, and lives are drastically changed. As we've said all along, we are "adoption facilitators."

Throughout this book, I have encouraged you to heed promptings from the Holy Spirit. Some of you might be frustrated with this kind of terminology and I don't want to leave you frustrated any longer.

When it comes to trying to discern when is the best time to talk to someone, I have found two forces at play at the same time. The Spirit's voice starts getting louder in my heart saying, "This is the time you've been waiting and praying for, the conversation is ripe for you to represent me—go for it." We could be talking about anything when I sense the Spirit say this to me, but usually we're talking about something that is very dear to the person's heart. It doesn't mean that we're necessarily having an emotionally-charged conversation. The second force I feel is the enemy trying to make me fearful about what is going to happen if I do go for it. The fear I feel is as much of an indicator to me as the Spirit's voice.

Are there times when I wish the Spirit's voice was louder and clearer? Absolutely! Are there times when I think He's leading me to ask a person a spiritual question, but I'm not 100 percent convinced of it? You bet! I'm not at all trying to say that I hear God's voice say to me loud enough for everyone to hear, "Chris, do this!" What I am

67

trying to say is that if I am living an obedient life, His voice becomes clearer over time.

The other key thing to remember is that God loves the heart and the efforts of someone who is trying to represent Him. If my motive is to love Him and love my friends enough to share with them, even if He wasn't prompting me like I thought He was, He will still take my efforts and bless them. He is so committed to people coming to himself that I can mess up a spiritual conversation and He'll still use it. The ones He can't use are the ones I never have because I'm waiting for a prompting from Him that is written in the sky for everyone in my city to read . . . and last time I checked, that's not His normal operating procedure!

So here I am, in my hair stylist's chair, in my friend's garage, at my kid's soccer game, at a restaurant over lunch. I'm feeling this increased level of nervousness because I know the Holy Spirit has directed the conversation in this way just so I would say something to my friends about Him. But I don't have a clue what to say. What do I do? Naturally use what they are talking about as a launching pad to talk about how your relationship with Christ has affected this subject in your life. Below are some examples of topics from which spiritual conversations are often launched along with a verse/passage you can refer to.

- For instance, if your friends are bouncing from one relationship to the next, looking for ultimate meaning in relationships, which they were never intended to provide, you can share with them that even though you've got great friends and (if applicable) a great marriage, it's your relationship with Christ that fills the relational tank in your life. As long as we look for other people to do that, we are ultimately going to be disappointed, but when we allow God to give us meaning, we will be filled like never before (Isa. 55:2–7).

- If your friends admit they are working at such a pace that their personal lives are beginning to suffer, maybe you can tell them that you used to be a workaholic yourself, but you woke up one day and realized you were doing what most people do (especially men)—trying to gain your purpose for living through your job. You finally came to the conclusion that it was a never-ending rat race. The constant drive for more (recognition, money, perks, etc.) was never going to end and eventually would leave you tired and frustrated. Instead, you started getting your sense of satisfaction and accomplishment from

69

your relationship with God through Jesus Christ, and ever since then, life hasn't been perfect, but the joy and peace in your life has skyrocketed (Ps. 127:2).

- If your friends say their financial situation is so tight they don't know how they are going to make it, which is the case for an ever growing number of Americans today who are just one missed paycheck away from financial ruin, you can talk about how living life by the financial principles laid out in the Bible has made a tremendous difference. Although you're taking in the same amount you always did, you're putting God first in your finances and ever since you've done that, God has provided in miraculous ways (Matt. 6:28–34).

- If your friends are experiencing loneliness at a level that is suffocating them, you can tell them about how Jesus has become your constant guide. How He promises *never* to leave you and how you feel Him with you each and every day. Does this mean that loneliness is never a visitor to your home anymore? Perhaps not, but when loneliness comes around, you now know what to do about it. You start reading your Bible or worshiping or doing the things that remind you of His love for you. And when you do that, everything changes (Prov. 18:24).

- If your friends admit to being controlled by something (eating, drugs, alcohol, or other addictive behaviors), you can tell them about the power that is available through Jesus Christ to overcome the addictive powers in our lives. You can share with them that the same power that raised Jesus from the dead is available to us (Eph. 1:19) to empower us to overcome anything! You can offer to help them find a Christian twelve step program and even attend a session or two with them so they don't feel like they're all alone.

- If your friends have made a drastic mistake, maybe had an affair or they were fired from their job for something they did wrong, etc., you can tell them how you have certainly blown it in the past, and have had times when you felt pretty awful about it. Then you can share with them about the amazing forgiveness you have found through your relationship with Jesus Christ (1 John 1:9).

Obviously I haven't covered all the possibilities here, just some of the more common ones. I am confident the Holy Spirit will give you the words to say when you need them. And remember, you can always come back in a later conversation and say, "Hey you know, I was thinking some more about our conversation the other day and here are some further thoughts I had about it."

After several spiritual conversations, the time will come when you sense that these people are seriously considering "crossing over the line" to believing in Jesus Christ. Perhaps they will make that decision sitting in a church service you've invited them to that is focused on people who are seeking spiritual truth. But often they will make that decision toward the end of a spiritual conversation you're having with them—if, as I've said throughout this chapter, you'll only ask. My good friend Jim Bogear says, "In life, if you never ask, the answer is always no."

It's as simple as saying, "So what do you think about all this? Do you think you're ready to open up your heart to a relationship with Jesus Christ?" If you feel like they need more information about what they are actually doing, you can show them some Scripture:

- Romans 3:23—Everyone has sinned.
- Romans 6:23—Sin creates a separation between us and God.
- Romans 5:8—God loved us enough to provide a way of forgiveness.
- Romans 10:9—Our responsibility is to confess and to receive.

You might have another simple explanation of the gospel you prefer, that's fantastic! Use whatever you're comfortable using. Just use something! Too many pre-Christians are left hanging because a friend wouldn't ask them if they were ready to cross over into believing faith.

What if they ask a question I don't know the answer to?

First of all, don't panic! What they are looking for first is your sincerity, not your ability to be a walking theological encyclopedia. Just say that they've asked a great question and that you'll do some research for them to get an answer. Later on you can do an online search for an answer to your friend's question, or call someone in your church who you think is knowledgeable about this issue and ask them for some help. Interestingly enough, I have found many times that when I come back with an educated answer, my friend is more impressed that I spent the time to do a little research than they were with the answer I brought them. Although this is not true 100 percent of the time, I have found that a majority of the time when someone asks a difficult theological question it is just a smoke screen so they don't have to deal with the issues they know they should deal with in their life. When I answer the smoke screen question, often we can get down to the issues that *really* matter to them.

YOU CAN DO THIS

I want to finish this chapter with a large dose of encouragement! You really can do this. All the power of heaven is behind you. Don't you dare let the enemy steal this joy from you. You are an adoption facilitator. You can radically increase other people's joy and your own in the process. So go for it! All of heaven is cheering you on toward getting in the game and playing the part you were destined by God to play.

KEY POINTS

- Ultimately we choose whether or not we are going to join God in being adoption facilitators.
- There are huge benefits that come our way when we join God in being adoption facilitators.
- The Spirit will prompt you.
- Don't be afraid to ask *the* question.
- You can do this!

DISCUSSION QUESTIONS

1. What do you think is the number one hindrance that keeps you from actually launching into a spiritual conversation? From what you have learned in this chapter, what specifically can you do about it?

2. How can you sense when you are receiving a prompting from the Holy Spirit?

3. Do you know someone in your life right now who God is prompting you to have a spiritual conversation with?

4. If your friends were ready to "cross over the line" and begin a relationship with Jesus Christ, how would you guide them through that process?

ACTION STEPS

1. Be attentive whenever non-Christian friends talk about an area of their lives that is leaving them dissatisfied.

2. See if the Holy Spirit doesn't prompt you at that point to make a statement about the difference being in a relationship with Jesus Christ has made in that area of your life.

3. Take them to a place in the Bible that talks about that area.

4. Ask your friends if they have any questions about being in a relationship with Christ that you could try and answer for them.

5. Ask them if they are ready to "cross over the line" and open up their lives to a relationship with Jesus Christ.

6. Lead them in a prayer—yes you can do this!—of your own words that they can repeat after you, expressing to God their desire to be forgiven and start a relationship with Him.

RESOURCES

- Bill Hybels and Mark Mittelberg—*Becoming a Contagious Christian*

- Bill Hybels—*A Walk Across the Room*

- Dallas Willard—*Hearing God: Developing a Conversational Relationship with God*

INVOLVE 5

> *The disciple is one who, intent upon becoming Christ-like and so dwelling in His "faith and practice," systematically and progressively rearranges his affairs to that end. By these decisions and actions, one enrolls in Christ's training, becomes His pupil or disciple. There is no other way.*
>
> Dallas Willard, *The Great Omission*

My first job out of college was working on staff at a (then) smaller church in Tucson, Arizona. Foothills Community Church had been planted just a year or so before I arrived. Jon and Connie Farmer, the lead church planters, were true pioneers. They moved to Tucson not knowing a soul in the community and carved out a ministry that has touched thousands of people's lives over the years. By the time this book goes to print, they will have planted a church in a neighboring community. When I arrived at Foothills, I was greeted with overwhelming warmth and acceptance by the entire congregation.

One family in particular, however, truly "took me in." Because the church was new and small, the most they were able to pay me was $600 a month. The rent on my apartment was $300, my car payment was $99 and my car insurance (being a single male under twenty-five) was $125. As you can tell, there wasn't much left over. As heavily involved laypeople, Gene and Joette knew my plight and adopted me into their family. They were forever including me in with their family's gatherings. Not just once in a while but several times a week. Obviously they were at a place in their family's development where this was healthy and not taxing on them. Although I was a long ways away from my own family, I never felt cheated of a family connection—Gene and Joette made sure of it.

THE NEXT STEP

By now we have spent time pouring into others' lives and asking God to do what only He can do. When we see a person's heart soften and then change right before our eyes, it's a miracle. Whenever this happens to the people I have been praying for and developing a friendship with, I am left in utter amazement at the fact that God gives me

an opportunity to join Him in this adventure.

Once your friends open up to a relationship with Christ, don't miss out on the opportunity to celebrate with them. Think about it—we celebrate so many things in a person's life: graduation, job promotions, anniversaries, birthdays, weddings, retirement. All of these events, as important as they seem at the time, have no eternal ramifications attached to them. The most important decision (by far) we will ever make, the one that has eternal significance, is the decision we make about Jesus Christ. So when our friends, coworkers, family members, etc. open up their hearts to a relationship with Jesus, that's a better reason than any to celebrate!

Take them out to dinner or have them over for their favorite meal. Bake a cake or serve them their favorite dessert. Make sure they know you are filled with joy along with the angels in heaven. Celebrating it in a big fashion and including anyone else who had a part in this process reinforces to your new brother or sister in Christ just how important a decision this really was. Put the date on your calendar so you can be sure to celebrate next year as well. Just as we keep track of our birthdays and anniversaries of various kinds, we should definitely keep track of when our friends "crossed over the line" into faith.

You might be tempted to think that after this celebration is over, your responsibility to your friends is over. Yes and no.

"Yes" in the sense that you should now ask the Heavenly Father to help you identify another person who you can begin to intercede for, intersect with, and invite to consider the claims of Jesus Christ. Don't stop this process in your life just because you've had the privilege of seeing one person come to Christ. Jesus didn't tell us to be His witnesses once and then go into permanent retirement in this area of our lives. In fact, the leading verse of the Great Commission is best translated from the original Greek language in this way:

> Jesus came and told his disciples, "I have been given all authority in heaven and on earth. Therefore, *go* and make disciples of all the nations, baptizing them in the name of the Father and the Son and the Holy Spirit." (Matt. 28:18–19, emphasis mine)

Jesus didn't see this as a one time event but as an ongoing regular aspect of our lives. "As you are going through life, make disciples."

82

Notice, Jesus didn't say, "Make Christians." It was never His intention to divide evangelism from discipleship. Jesus assumed that we would not only help people come into a relationship with Jesus Christ, but that we would also help them in their growth toward a dynamic relationship with Him. This is where the fifth step in the process comes in: Involve them in a deepening relationship with Jesus and His church.

When an emotionally healthy mother gives birth to a son or daughter, their natural instinct is to begin to nurture this child—to care for it and make sure that it not only survives but that it thrives. Emotionally healthy mothers do not abandon their child to care for themselves because an infant has no capacity to do this.

In the same way, emotionally healthy Christians do not abandon their friends once they have opened up their lives to a relationship with Jesus Christ, neither do they make their new brother or sister in Christ totally dependent on them for spiritual nurturing. Mature Christians help their new Christian friends find the right mix between depending on them, depending on other Christians and depending on Christ, with the eventual goal that they will move ever more toward being dependent on Christ for their spiritual growth and health.

A PRACTICAL GUIDE TO DISCIPLESHIP

The following guide is just that, a guide. Use it and adapt it to your friends and their situations.

Identify

The last thing we want to do is to make the same mistake so many other Christians have made by cocooning themselves in a Christian culture. So encourage them, right from the start, to begin to identify people in their lives who need to come into a relationship with Jesus Christ. As people who have just come to Christ, their lives are probably filled with relationships with non-Christian people; people God would love to know.

Encourage them to write out their testimony. It doesn't have to be long, just a quick synopsis of how they came into a relationship with Jesus Christ and why they decided to become a Christ-follower. Writing it down will accomplish a number of things: (1) For some, it helps to solidify their decision when they commit it to paper; (2) it will help them know what to say when their non-Christian friends ask about the changes they are observing in their friend's life; and (3) it can be used the day the person is baptized.

The sooner they start the "identify, intercede, intersect, invite, and involve" process themselves, the sooner they will feel the joy of being used by God in a dynamic way.

Baptism

Encourage your friends to be baptized. Help them understand baptism by sharing with them that opening up our hearts to a relationship with Jesus Christ is a very private event between us and God and maybe one other person. Baptism is the celebration of that event. Baptism is like a wedding ring—it's the outward symbol of the commitment we make in our hearts.

Here are some points that might be helpful to you as you talk to your friends about making this important step:

1. Baptism does not make you a believer in Jesus Christ; it shows that you already are one!

"We were therefore buried with him through baptism into death in order that, just as Christ was raised from the dead through the glory of the Father, we too may live a new life!" (Rom. 6:4 NIV).

85

2. Baptism does not "save" you, only your faith in Christ does.

"For by grace you have been saved, through faith . . . it is the gift of God, not as a result of works, so that no one may boast" (Eph. 2:8–9 NASB).

3. Baptism is a symbol of Christ's burial and resurrection.

"Christ died for our sins . . . He was buried, and He was raised from the dead" (1 Cor. 15:3–4).

"For you were buried with Christ when you were baptized. And with him you were raised to new life" (Col. 2:12 NIV).

4. Baptism is a symbol of your new life as a Christian.

"Anyone who belongs to Christ has become a new person. The old life is gone; a new life has begun!" (2 Cor. 5:17).

Perhaps your friends were raised in a tradition where they were baptized as an infant. If this is the case, they will undoubtedly ask you if they should be baptized again. My response to this is always, "I recommend you get baptized again. This doesn't devalue a prior experience—it simply reflects your desire to be baptized in the same way Jesus was, as an adult." Often people are concerned about what will happen if their parents hear they are getting baptized. "Is this going to make them feel like what they did wasn't good enough?" My answer to this very valid concern for some is to be forthright and tell their parents that they're getting baptized, but that this baptism doesn't nullify at all their infant baptism. When their parents baptized them as an infant, their goal in that baptism was that their son or daughter would grow up and develop a relationship with God. This baptism is a celebration that their parent's prayer on that day has now become a reality.

Encourage your friends to be baptized as soon as possible. This will keep them from putting it off and never getting around to actually doing it.

Prayer

Chances are, your friends have been praying for a while already. According to Barna, in a typical week, 66 percent of unchurched people pray compared to 84 percent of all adults who do so. But new Christians want to know how they can make their prayer time more effective. You can help them by explaining to them that prayer is simply talking with God—and they can talk to God about anything! The problems they're facing, questions about their future, times when they need wisdom. The Bible promises God listens *and* responds when we pray!

"Anyone who is having troubles should pray" (James 5:13 NCV).

"Don't worry about anything; instead, pray about everything. Tell God what you need, and thank him for all he has done. Then you will experience God's peace, which exceeds anything we can understand. His peace will guard your hearts and minds as you live in Christ Jesus" (Phil. 4:6–7).

"The LORD is close to everyone who prays to him" (Ps. 145:18 NCV).

"If you need wisdom, ask our generous God, and he will give it to you" (James 1:5).

Bible Reading

The Bible can appear intimidating to new Christians. They often think, "It's such a big book, where do I begin?" Encourage them that for now, start reading the book of James in the New Testament. But before doing that, purchase for them or help them purchase a Bible that uses language they can easily understand. All too often new Christians will pick up a King James Version they were given when they were baptized as an infant. Reading this will probably only frustrate them and leave them feeling like the Bible is not truly relevant to their life today.

Once they have a modern translation of the Bible, help them understand the layout of their Bible. Show them where the index is. Show them the Old and New Testaments. Help them find the book of Psalms and encourage them to read that when they're not having the best of days.

By far, the very best gift you can give them when it comes to understanding the Bible is to agree to do an entry level Bible study with them. There are many quality ones on the market today. A trip to your local Bible book store should provide ample resources for you and your friends to study for four to six weeks together.

Fellowship and Small Group

Invite your friends to join you at your small group or join them at a small group they are interested in attending.

Life-change discipleship often happens best in small groups. When people enter into community, they put themselves in a place where they can learn how to apply the teaching they are hearing. They also put themselves in a place where accountability can take place. It's one thing for someone to say, "I am a Christian, but I still have an anger problem." It's another thing all together to have people praying for us and asking us how we dealt with our anger during the preceding week. The primary way we experience God's love is through others. Simply put, Christ will not be formed in us unless we are in community.

> God's aim in human history is the creation of an all inclusive community of loving persons with himself included as its prime sustainer and most glorious inhabitant.
>
> Dallas Willard

Discipleship

When it comes right down to it, our ultimate goal is that we help our now Christian friends to find the tools necessary in life so that Christ would be fully formed in them.

One of my very favorite writers in the area of discipleship is Dallas Willard. In the first chapter of his book, *The Great Omission,* he talks clearly about the price we pay when we refuse to make discipleship a priority in our lives. He calls this phenomenon: *nondiscipleship.* "Nondiscipleship costs abiding peace, a life penetrated by love, faith that sees everything in the light of God's overriding governance for good, hopefulness that stands firm in the most discouraging of circumstances, power to do what is right and withstand the forces of evil. In short, nondiscipleship costs exactly the abundance of life Jesus said He came to bring in John 10:10."

This is much too high a price to pay. Wise students of Christ will immerse themselves and encourage their non-Christian friends to immerse themselves in red. What I mean by that is the "red letters" found in many Bibles—the words of Jesus in the Gospels.

It is not uncommon for me to read the Bible through in a year. I typically follow a program I made up for myself five years or so ago that takes me through the Old Testament in less than six months and then allows me to spend the rest of the year in the New Testament. But by far, the times when I am most impacted, the times when my life is challenged by and changed through the Holy Spirit, are the times when I slowly read through the words of Jesus. This is particularly true when I am reading the Sermon on the Mount in Matthew 5–7. Often all I need is just to read a verse or two and the Holy Spirit has plenty of things He can say to me through them.

Encouraging your friends to hang out in the red letters and then get together with you once a week to debrief what they are reading and learning would be a fantastic way to help them get started on the right foot to becoming a disciple of Jesus.

IN CLOSING

Often people ask how they can know God's will for their life. While it would be foolish for me to speculate about how to best live out the kingdom in certain areas of your life I know nothing about, I do know that God wants you introduce as many as you can to the love of Jesus Christ. Follow the five steps I have laid out in this book and I guarantee you a front row seat in the best concert you could ever attend. Yes, the stakes are high. Yes, the demands are occasionally great. But the payoff is worth it, and it continues long past this life all the way into eternity. Don't miss out!

- Once people become Christ-followers we have a responsibility to help them grow deeper in their relationship.

- Baptism is a public proclamation of inner change.

- Christian community is the best environment for spiritual growth.

- Jesus commanded us to make disciples, not just Christians.

INVOLVE

DISCUSSION QUESTIONS

1. Think back to when you were a brand new Christian, what are some things you wish someone would have shared with you to make your pursuit of Christ easier from the beginning?

2. What are the spiritual disciplines or habits that you have incorporated in your life that seem to help you grow the most in your relationship with Christ? (Understand, these may not be the same ones that will help your friends grow in their relationships with Christ the most. For instance, both prayer and reading the Bible are important in a Christian's life, but while one person may grow closer to God through reading large chunks of the Bible at a time, another person might grow more through prayer and fasting.)

93

3. Why do you think small groups can be such an effective means of life change in the life of a Christ-follower?

4. Does your local church have a system in place to help new Christians get off on the right foot in their relationship with Christ? If not, could this be an area God is calling you to involve yourself with?

ACTION STEPS

1. As your friends have come to a saving relationship with Jesus Christ, intentionally guide them deeper into the life of a disciple.

2. Explain the act of baptism to them and encourage them to do it as quickly as they can.

3. Set up a time to study the Bible with your friends.

4. Pray continually for your friends and ask God to help you identify others around that need to know about Him.

RESOURCES

- John Ortberg—*The Life You've Always Wanted*
- Dallas Willard—*The Divine Conspiracy*
- Dallas Willard—*The Great Omission*
- Dietrich Bonhoeffer—*Life Together*
- Ken Heer—*A Good Start*